To Jen,
YOU
RULE!

Thomas
Baldrick

The Hopes and Dreams
of 21st Century Children

By

Thomas Baldrick

Popular Demand Book Company, Ltd
Philadelphia, PA

www.popdbooks.com

Published by Popular Demand Book Company, LTD
P.O. Box 16216
Philadelphia, PA 19114-6216

Publisher's Cataloging-in-Publication Data
Baldrick, Thomas.
      Kids rule! : the hopes and dreams of 21st century children / Thomas Baldrick. -- Philadelphia, Penn. : Popular Demand Book Company, LTD. 2001.
          p. cm.
      ISBN 0-9708121-0-8

      1. Children--Quotations. 2. Parenting--Quotations. I. Title. II. Hopes and dreams of 21st century children

PN6328.C5 B35   2001   2001086443
808.882/0083   dc--21   CIP

03   02   01   00 • 5   4   3   2   1

Printed in Singapore

About the author photo by Karen Lee Ensley

In Memory Of
EVAN
"Little King Of The Binky"

I wish I could have watched you walk.

I wish I could have heard you talk.

I wish I could have seen you grow.

I wish you didn't have to go.

Thank you for bringing joy to the world for 363 days.
I miss you.

About the Author

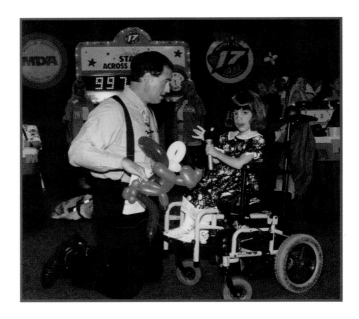

Thomas Baldrick would first like to thank you for helping needy children! A donation will be made to children's charities with every sold copy of the book. Though just a kid at heart in a man's body, this author has done quite well in the world of grownups since graduating from Temple University with a degree in Radio-Television-Film.

He is a 6-time Emmy-Award winning television host, reporter and producer/writer. A passion for helping children and charities can be seen in many of his television credits including work with "The Jerry Lewis Labor Day Telethon," "Habitat For Humanity," "Toys For Tots" and "The United Negro College Fund Telethon." Thomas also writes centerpiece feature stories for Metro, a daily newspaper in Philadelphia.

He has served as a longtime volunteer giving his time to little ones at The Children's Hospital of Philadelphia. Spiritual, sensitive, funny and hardworking. Thomas is single and a hometown native of "The City of Brotherly Love," Philadelphia, PA. For more information visit www.baldrick.com or email him at thomas@baldrick.com.

"Thomas Baldrick's book gleans the innocence and vulnerability of childhood. Upon reading it, you will discover that today's lesson is to listen to the voices of <u>our</u> children. Tomorrow's lesson will be to use love and wisdom to create new possibilities for them."

Lynda Doran, educator

Table of Contents

So Where ARE My Kids?

If I've heard the questions once, I've heard them a thousand times. People who've never before seen the magic of me with children ask the same questions: 1. "So how many kids do YOU have?" 2. "Why hasn't some nice girl snapped you up yet?" For the record, the correct answers are: 1. None. 2. I don't know.

Sometimes, I say my kids are with my wife. So where is she you ask? How should I know? I haven't met her yet! There is another comment I always hear when a parent is surprised by their child's instant bond with me. They say, "My child isn't usually like this with other people!" I just laugh and say, "I know." And I do. For some reason, I have been blessed with a special gift of connecting with children. Boys or girls, black or white, sick or healthy, kids just seem to know I care. Whether it's a screaming baby needing comfort, a messy bottom needing a change, little toddlers needing attention or bigger ones needing a laugh, kids just know I care. Sometimes, when I'm holding a sick child in the hospital, it hurts when people who thought I was a caring doctor or loving father, look at me differently when they learn I'm just a single guy who volunteers. The way I look at my life with kids is simple. Since I've yet to be blessed with marriage or fatherhood, my mission on earth is to love lots of children!

In 1992, I became one of the television hosts of "The Philadelphia Mummers New Year's Day Parade." This popular event is a tradition as "Philly-like" as soft pretzels and cheese steaks. My inspiration for this book came through a letter written to me by a viewer. Lynda Doran, a gifted teacher at the Whitman Elementary School in Turnersville, NJ, wrote, *"every time I see you on TV, I get the feeling you love children. I hope you don't mind, but my 2nd grade class had an assignment to write letters. They've written to you. It would be great if you could write back to the class."* I didn't. I wrote to each child. Then, I visited the class. We had a ball! Ms. Doran told me, *"There's such a gift in your writing."* After a few hours of her words playing over and over in my head, the idea for this book came like a lightning bolt from heaven. I knew it just had to be done.

My goal was to feature the joy and innocence of children in a book for them and about them. Therefore, all of the little angels included were no older than 4th grade. Along the path to publication, I connected with nearly 15,000 children from Buffalo to Bosnia-Hercegovina! I made it safe for kids to open their hearts and share what was most important. Many times my heart was warmed. Other times it was broken when a child would ask, "You mean you really want to know what I think? No one has ever asked me that before."

I said there were no right or wrong answers. There were no good or bad answers. I dared not even change their spelling, grammar or artwork. My feeling was, "Who am I to mess with perfection?" I simply told kids, "I want to remind grownups that *kids rule the world!*" The response was always the same. Their sudden chants created the only title that fit the book. "*Kids Rule!*" Kids offer the best chance to change the world over the long haul. They are great teachers about things like love, laughter, simplicity and curiosity. But too often their innocence gets lost or stolen far too early in life.

This book shows many kids do what they see and say what they hear. Grownups need to teach more *by example*. How can be kids be expected to understand problem solving and conflict resolution when they see grownups screaming at one another in traffic, suing one another in courts and even shooting one another on streets?

The needs and feelings of children are too often left behind. When a troubled kid makes news, everyone wonders what was going on his head. By then, it's too late. This book is offered as a celebration of the beauty of children and to shine a spotlight on their little hopes, dreams, needs and cries for help. *Now* is the time.

My Native American teacher, White Buffalo, would often shout, "Take a chance people!" And so I have. What began as a solo mission, ended in a total team effort. I was truly blessed with the help of principals, teachers, parents and children. Special thanks to my kid loving friends: Lucy Butterbaugh, Vincent Cardile, Sister Mildred Chesnavage, Ted Derr, Charlie Donnelly, Lynda Doran, Michele Farina, Kathy Gendelman, Diane Jelen, Jerrold Jenkins, Lisa Liney, Jeanne Meredith, Lou Panza, Betty Pehlman, Bob Pfeilsticker, Joan Rosenburgh, Richard Slusarski, Peggy Stengel, and Dave Willauer.

I thank The Maui Writers Conference for providing me the opportunity to be discovered and for me to discover the powerful writer inside. I honor my cousin, Stephen Druding for his artistic creativity and undying support. Ditto for my gift of a literary agent, Rita Rosenkranz. She made me a better writer. They all helped to make this a better book. Finally, I praise my God, His Blessed Mother and their colleagues for the love and guidance I needed to finish the book.

I hope what you read on these pages touches the child within you and opens your sacred human heart. Then, you can open wider to the sacred human hearts of children in your family, your neighborhood and your world. Every child is a precious gift. May the hopes and dreams of all us children come true.

Namaste! (The God in me bows to the God in you.)

With love,

Thomas Baldrick

Priceless.COMments

Upon reviewing *KIDS RULE*, popular author, Bernie S. Siegel, M.D. wrote, *"What every child needs is a good listener. Read and listen to their message!"* I can't think of better advice as you begin this book.

In Bernie's *Prescriptions for Living*, he writes about the wisdom of children and how they teach us about love, honesty and understanding feelings. The following pages provide a platform for such simple but sound teachings.

I wanted to find a way to help children everywhere. I used a simple approach to the complex issue. I got children to reveal their most important wishes. Featuring them in a book, gives the world another chance to learn what's going on inside these little wonders. By doing so, maybe, just maybe, more children will get their needs met.

I call this a "potato chip book." It's tough to open and read from just one child. While many of the entries are funny, the real juicy way to read this book is to stop along the way and allow yourself to be touched by what a child felt. If you do this, you'll understand the quotes on the cover of the book.

Enjoy, as they share the priceless issues at the top of their little priority lists!

I wish I could become a lawyer or a garbageman.

Jacob–Age 8

I wish to live in the King of Purssia Mall.

Kaeley–Age 10

I wish for my mom to clean my room now.

Josh–Age 7

I wish I had munny to by close for the girls in my daddys books.

Christopher–Age 6

I wish That my friend Madeline to come back to America because I miss right now because she's in Maryland because her dad got a better job.

Miranda–Age 8

I wish that all the stuff comes out of my nails.

William–Age 6

I wish that I could never get timeout!

Melody–Age 7

I wish the sun comes out on my dad's birthday.

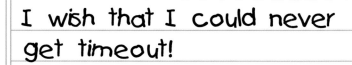

Kathleen–Age 8

I wish my enemies would
be nicer and kinder.

Emily–Age 9

I wish Nicholas B.
will move tomorrow.

Casey–Age 9

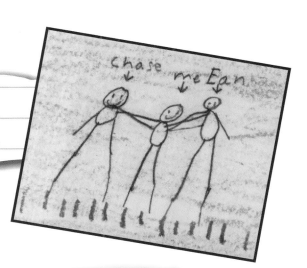

I wish that Cory could do
some of my chores and that
I could sleep over Rachael's
house not staceys house.

Robyn–Age 9

I wish everyone in the world
would have an edgeacation.

Emily–Age 8

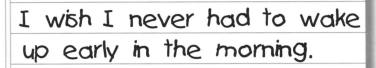

I wish I never had to wake up early in the morning.

Caitlyn–Age 10

I wish to go bakkc in time and meet stonewall Jackson.

Jackson–Age 9

I wish I was cool.

Tara–Age 10

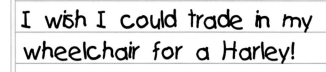

I wish I could trade in my wheelchair for a Harley!

Alexa–Age 7

A Whole Lot
Of Munny

It's tough enough for kids to spell or even say Rockefeller, let alone become one. It's just as hard for them to learn the Presidents of the United States, let alone whose faces are on which bills, how much they're worth and more importantly, how you get them to buy cool stuff!

"The American Dream" waits for no one. Most kids learn at an early age that money can buy power. They want to be rich as much as adults. They just have a different view on how much is enough!

Enjoy the kids as they try to make sense of dollars and cents!

I wish I won the jackpot so I could give it to my mom.

Samantha–Age 9

I wish I had 99 billion dollars and 82 cents.

Megan–Age 6

I wish I could become richer than Bill Gates.

Jacob–Age 8

I wish I could be a rich (but neat) person.

Lauren–Age 10

I wish for $10,000,000,000.97

Shannon–Age 11

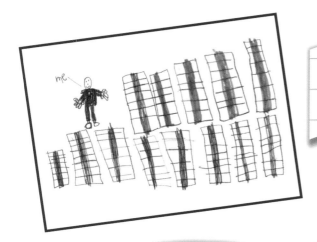

I wish I had 81 dolrs.

Maria–Age 7

I wish to be queen of the world and have a castle atached to a manchin and have 36 million dollers.

Natalie–Age 7

I wish to have my head on a dollar bill.

Mark–Age 9

From Here To Maternity

I'd like to propose a toast! To young love and the birth of new ideas!

I wish to have
a boy friend.

Madeline–Age 3

I wish to get marryed
to a cute man.

Tajah–Age 8

I wish all the
girls would go
crazy over me.

Andrew–Age 10

I wish I had no wife
when I grow up.

Joey–Age 9

I wish for Jesus to give my mom a baby brother or my mom to buy me a jeep.

Antonella–Age 6

I wish for a motorbike and I want a brother. When I told my mom she said she will buy me a motorbike.

Ivana–Age 3

I wish that my dog will meat a girl dog so they will have pupies.

Natalie–Age 7

Okay, Maybe I Can't Spell Veterinarian . . . But . . .

While writing this book, I went to Maine to produce a story for television. There, I had the thrill of my first up close and personal encounter with a Bull Moose as he enjoyed a hearty roadside breakfast of berries and greens. It was so exciting for me!

Moose can be rather cranky during mating season, so I'm glad he either wasn't threatened by my presence or didn't find my scent appealing! Regardless, on my flight home, I was still in awe of my meeting with Mr. Moose on the loose. It was a very large gift in having one more chance to relive child-like feelings toward animals.

I wish my mom
would let me
get a rat.

Liz–Age 10

I wish for a turtle.
I wish there was
no turtle soup.

Kelli–Age 7

I wish my dog will
never get his foot
stuk in my bike.

Alisa–Age 9

I wish I had a pony
named Bob.

Richard–Age 10

I wish I had an isand full of dinosaurs and a helicopter pad in my backyard so I can go to the island.

Joseph—Age 7

I wish I had a guinny pig.

Christina—Age 8

I wish I had a fluffy, fuzzy, cute, sweat, little, golden retriver puppy.

Kelly—Age 6

I wish my cat back because she died on my birthday.

Abigail—Age 8

From Power Players To Power Brokers

Parenting isn't for babies! Successful moms and dads have a great deal of responsibility. They must be fair, honest, flexible, willing to give and take, willing to trust, willing to sacrifice and committed to communicating with children, even when it may not be easy. Oh yeah, successful parents also have to do all of this while trying to maintain a career or any kind of personal life.

There is a great deal of power in setting healthy boundaries. Parents need to set aside time to do something for themselves. Make no exceptions unless it is what you want. It works! Whether it's making a date with your spouse, reading and relaxing, exercising, or visiting with friends, you can do it once you decide you are worthy!

I always remind people of pre-flight instructions from an airline. If the oxygen masks are released, they tell you to place your mask on first. Then, you are to help a child or elderly person. This simply means you have to take care of yourself first so you are at your best to provide care to those who rely on you.

Loving and secure adults help to grow trustworthy kids. Kids love empowerment over control. Just ask them! Believing in a child can help that little person to become powerful. The words and actions of adults create lifelong images and beliefs in children.

Please, make them positive!

I wish we could drive cars and kids could boss parents around.

Carolann—Age 8

I wish earth lived in peace and very little dinosaurs, the ones that did no damage, ruled the world.

Joseph—Age 7

I wish to live in Egyptian times and be an emporer.

Stephen—Age 11

I wish I was the boss of the world and told my mom and dad wha to do.

Kathleen—Age 7

Home "Not So" Sweet Home

A home is not the dwelling where a child lives. Such places are called houses, apartments, etc. A real home for a child is being with the ones they love and who love them. Home is the team with whom they sometimes win and other times lose . . . sometimes laugh and other times cry . . . sometimes fight for and other times fight against.

Home is where a child craves to be seen, heard, nurtured and yes, even disciplined. (This does not mean they ever want to be physically hurt or attacked with words!) Not all children have the home field advantage. Unfortunately, for some, home IS where the heart is.

I wish my dad would be
alive again and my mom
would be happy again.

Toniann–Age 9

I wish my
family would
love me more.

Alyse–Age 8

I wish I did
not have to
go home.

Joshua–Age 6

I wish and I really wish
my brother would stop
calling me names and
hateing me.

Nicole–Age 11

I wish for my dad and mom to stop fighting and my brother to stop beting me up.

Nikki–Age 8

I wish my mom came back to my dad.

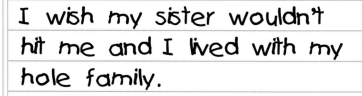

Randy–Age 6

I wish my sister wouldn't hit me and I lived with my hole family.

Kathleen–Age 10

I wish I could meet my real dad and my mom could get a job and buy us a house.

Krystal–Age 7

Into The Mouths Of Babes

Studies show Americans are getting fatter. Imagine what we'd be like if kids ruled the world and it did rain candy and milkshakes! Watching your weight is good. Watching what you eat and how much of it you eat is better!

I wish there would be
enough food for everyone.

Kenneth–Age 9

I wish I could eat all the
junk food I want.

Courtney–Age 10

I wish I would
never have to
eat tuna again!

Brittany–Age 9

I wish I could
eat in my room.

Shannon–Age 7

I wish for blueberry ice-cream
and all the other ice creams
mixed together and I would
eat them until I got a
headache. It would realy hurt.

Kirsten–Age 7

I'll Trade You a Safety and a Crossing Guard For a Manager and a Bodyguard!

While it's true, fame and fortune do have their price. It's also true most kids are more than willing to pay it. Get ready to hear from young ones who gladly choose fame over phonics!

I wish I was a
movie star.

Brandon–Age 7

I wish Stone Cold and the
under taker would be my
bote guard.

Jonathan–Age 10

I wish to live in
disneyworld with
my kids. I wish
for when I get
older for the
whole world to
know me.

kelly–Age 10

I wish I could meet
Celine Dion and
never had to go to
the dentist.

Ashley–Age 9

I'll Trade You a Safety and a Crossing Guard For a Manager and a Bodyguard!

I wish I was a firegirl and meet N'SNKE.

Erin–Age 8

I wish to live with Brittany Spears and be the smartest purson in the world.

Eric–Age 9

I wish that I could be famous so that after I die many people will remember me.

Madalyn–Age 9 1/2

I wish I could make a great stupendis picture.

Briannon–Age 8

I'll Trade You a Safety and a Crossing Guard For a Manager and a Bodyguard!

For Score . . . And Many Years From Now

   "Winning is the only thing"** is the wrong attitude to teach kids. Enjoyment and teamwork seem to be far better goals for little leaguers than victory at all costs. As for role models, good parents always beat great athletes.

I wish I could be the first person to dunk from the 3-point line.

Cliff–Age 9

I wish to take over Bobby Kenevel a dare devel.

Bobby–Age 11

My wish is to have a good coach for basketball.

Colleen–Age 8

I wish I could race Jeff Gordon and that I would never see a tornado again.

Andrew–Age 8

I wish I would never do skydiving.

Michael–Age 8

I wish to compeat with Mia Hamm and be the first girl to climb the Grand Canyon.

Sara–Age 11

I wish to be a famiss football player.

Matthew–Age 9

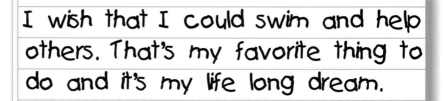

I wish that I could swim and help others. That's my favorite thing to do and it's my life long dream.

Seana–Age 10

Nobel Prize . . . No Problem!

Using your imagination is good. Paying attention to your inner voice is good. (Yes, we all have them!) Listen to yourself. Remember, every great invention, successful business and contribution to society begins with an idea!

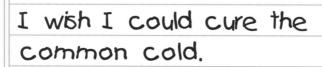

I wish I could cure the common cold.

James—Age 10

I wish that a robot could do my homework.

Mitch—Age 10

I wish I could invent something useful.

Charles—Age 7

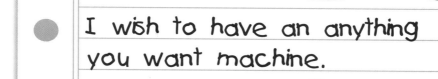

I wish to have an anything you want machine.

Matthew—Age 9

School Days . . . School Daze

In doing this book, I saw the Herculean effort required by today's schoolteachers and administrators. We all know too well that schools are where many problems at home are expressed by children.

In my visits to schools, I've come across many "classroom caretakers" who provide students with love, attention, structure and an education. These teachers do make a difference. Their job is not at all an easy one. It is like they must make a daily climb up a slippery hill. None of the teachers I know are getting rich financially, though they are indeed worthy. The class in which the kids rule the schools is now in session.

I wish I didn't have to be in my enemies class.

Kathleen–Age 10

I want to be a teacher. I want to yell at kids too.

Andrianna–Age 7

I wish I can go to Harvard University.

Kara Marie–Age 10

I wish for no homework and to have recess all day.

Vincent–Age 8

I wish I always have
Miss D. for a teacher.

Jessica–Age 9

I wish that my
teacher couldn't
get any prettier
than she is now.

I'm so
happy!!!

Kelly–Age 9

I wish I could
quit honors
math.

Colleen–Age 9

I wish school was only one day
and summer was all year long
ecept for on the school day.

Keith–Age 10

Now I Know My ABC's . . . Tell Me When I'm CEO!

One should **never** squash another's dreams. Don't listen to anyone who calls your dreams silly or stupid. Don't let their fears become yours. Every single person can be whatever they want. To be successful in life, you simply have to do what you enjoy (as long as it doesn't hurt anyone!)

Set goals. Don't be afraid to ask for help. You'll be surprised at how many helpful people the universe will place on your path. Besides, the worst that can happen is someone might say "no." If they do, you still didn't lose anything, did you? Don't take one no for an answer. Remember, when one door closes, another opens.

Be determined. Stay positive. Everything is possible. I'll bet success stories like Bill Gates, Oprah Winfrey, Tiger Woods and N SYNC are glad they didn't let people stop them from reaching for the stars! Follow your passion. Good things will happen (and not always the way you expected!)

I wish I could be a business man and own a dodge durango.

Kevin–Age 10 1/2

I wish I was the first kid president.

Patrick–Age 10

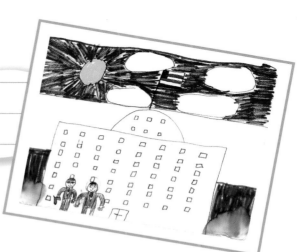

I wish for people to come to me when I sell things.

Alexander–Age 6

I wish I could be the first astranot with diabetes.

Pat–Age 11

I wish for to be a arcetant and builder.

Christos–Age 10

I wish to own a cafe.

Emily–Age 9

I wish that I owned an ice cream truck.

Brittany–Age 10

I wish I can get a jod!

Alexandra–Age 7

One Size Does NOT Fit All

There may be nothing we take for granted more than the human body. In the mere blink of an eye, it performs millions of extraordinary tasks in a very ordinary way. If you surf the web or read books, you'll learn in a heartbeat that the body is the most amazing tool we have.

No matter how you view or treat your body, it does its best to serve you. You are its master. Do you love or even like your body? Can you stand before a mirror and look at yourself for a second without seeing only what you think are flaws?

Take a moment to find one body part you do love. Give thanks for all it does for you and how it makes you feel. Choose different body parts to learn about and love. You should become happier, healthier and more aware of this unique gift. Your body IS your buddy.

I wish I could fly and be invisable.

Nicole–Age 8

I wish that I wouldn't have asthma and that I wouldn't have worts.

Corey–Age 9

I wish for my sister to get better and not have her disease.

Ryan–Age 9

I wish I were a boy.

Kimmie–Age 6

I wish I could walk like the other kids.

Shantel–Age 6

I wish I was the priteaist gril in the wrld and can war the most butaphl dres.

Alexandra–Age 6

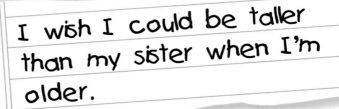

I wish that my foot didn't get covered in poison ivy in the summer.

Emily–Age 10

I wish I could be taller than my sister when I'm older.

Lindsay–Age 9

I want to be 2 inches tall.

Katie–Age 9

Pages For The Ages

Wouldn't it be great to spend your whole life saying "Wow! I don't feel old!" In this section, the little dears speak of years. It begs the question, "At what age do our feelings on growing older turn negative?"

With age comes experience. There is no greater teacher than experience. It is a gift much like love, that keeps on giving. Just think, when you turn 50 you will have all of the memories and experiences of a 1, 2, 10, 20, 30, 40 and 50 year old! Getting older can mean getting better. You can use all of your experiences to grow wiser, happier and more at peace with who you are.

Maybe you can try to live life as one never-ending collection of moments like "right now." Living in the present moment, "*the now*" is the only way to truly live life to the fullest. Remember, tomorrow (or even later today) is promised to no one.

I wish that all kids would get their ears perse at age 8.

Holly–Age 8

I wish I was a gronup.

Brandee–Age 6

I wish I could have 4 kids when I'm 14.

Sarah–Age 8

I wish that my mom won't die until I'm 30.

Kaitlyn–Age 9

I wish my dad wasnt' old and culd run. He is fat.

Brianna–Age 7

I wish I was 12.

Caitlin–Age 11

I wish all the poeple in the world could stay the age that they are this year forever.

Colleen–Age 9

I wish that I would have a long life.

Alexis–Age 9

I wish I will win one more champinship for soccer before I'm 11. I wish I would die when I turn 11.

Brian–Age 9

Kids 2 Heaven

Kids seem to view God as a friend with a real cool job. I also love their awe and lack of fear when speaking of God. After all, fear is an opposite of love.

Kids in little heavenly bodies are a great way to boost anyone's faith in a higher power. You may find it easy to see a creator in the eyes or smile of an infant or small child.

I wish god is haveing a good time.

Shelby–Age 7

I wish I had a guardian angel.

Corey–Age 11

I wish that God was still alive.

Katie–Age 10

I wish I could visit heaven for one week.

Kimberly–Age 10

I wish I was at the last supper.

Patrick–Age 7

I want to visit Medjugorje again because there are many beautiful statues of saints and angels. I also hope that God makes my birthday come as soon as possible.

Christina–Age 7

I wish that God and Jesus lived with me.

Joseph–Age 9

I wish I could switch places with GOD for one day.

Kaitlyn–Age 8

Sticks & Stones May Break My Bones But People Break My Heart

Hello out there! Can you see us? Can you hear us? Can anyone hear us? We are just little people trying to find our way and we often feel lost and scared. Sometimes we don't even know if we are good enough for anybody or anything.

Please help us! Teach us! Don't just yell at us! Be with us! We don't understand this once in a while thing grownups call "quality time." We just know if we're with you when it counts.

Love us! Show us we are special! We promise to love you back! We always hear grownups say "Time is money." If this is true, being with us will make your life rich!"

Sincerely,

21st Century Children

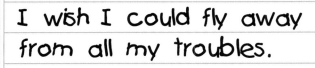

I wish I could fly away from all my troubles.

Kimberly–Age 10

I wish I had a friend.

Sarah–Age 8

I wish there were no more grown-ups.

Taylor–Age 6

I wish that someone will like me when I get older.

Heather–Age 9

I wish that someone would love + care for me.

Santina–Age 7

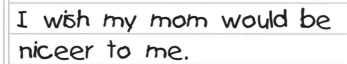

I wish my mom would be niceer to me.

Nick–Age 7

I wish people wouldn't pick on me.

Racile–Age 10

I wish for people like me and not hate me.

Alexander–Age 10

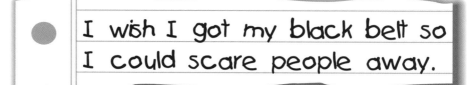

I wish I got my black belt so I could scare people away.

Charlie–Age 8 1/2

Little Bodies . . . BIG Eyes & Ears

Maybe cute little kids wouldn't be so cute if their eyes and ears grew faster than the rest of their bodies. On the other hand, maybe oversized eyes and ears would remind everyone that kids develop their senses of seeing and hearing early in life!

As you know, this book is loaded with information gathering specialists, all under the age of 12! I'll admit with television, movies, the internet and two income families, it's tough to shield kids in the 21st Century. Keeping them busy in social activities doesn't stop them from seeing and hearing this world of ours.

Communication is the answer. Now more than ever, kids and adults need to talk with each other and listen to each other and share their feelings and concerns.

I have a friend who talks with her pre-school kids about what they see and hear from television, videos, other kids and grownups. She talks openly with them in real terms, on their level. Believe you me, it works!

I have another friend who is a single father. He enjoys a special relationship with his young son. They love each other and respect each other very much. He makes sure he praises his son when he does something good. He also helps to correct him when he does something wrong. He doesn't yell at the boy. He *corrects* him. He simply teaches him the right way.

What's really great about this rare relationship is that the boy is also allowed to do the same things with his father. They feel it is done with love and respect. They learn from each other, help each other and share a wonderful gift.

I wish that everyone wouldn't take drugs and smoke because that is how everyone get's killed.

Jennifer–Age 9

I wish that there would be no violance in the world.

Lauren–Age 10

I wish people would think that all people are the same.

Patrick–Age 11

I wish my mom and dad would stop holiring at me.

William–Age 9

I wish not to
die of murder.

Eric–Age 10

I wish I would
dream about
good things.

Jonathan–Age 10

I wish to stop
the killing.

Christine–Age 10

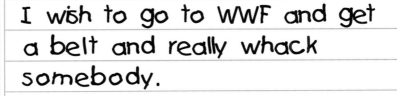

I wish to go to WWF and get
a belt and really whack
somebody.

Josh–Age 9

Little Bodies . . . BIG HEARTS

The children in this section have big eyes and ears. They also have big hearts. They are concerned with life's treasures that have no dollar signs attached to them. These little leaders of tomorrow are already making a difference in changing our world for the better . . . today. Savor this proof that there is indeed hope for humanity.

I wish people are liked
for who they are.

Lauren–Age 9

I wish people had
everything that
they need.

Tara–Age 7

I wish I could make
all the people on
earth happy.

Patrick–Age 6

I wish that the
whole world can
learn math and be
kind to eachother.

Poneviliy–Age 8

I wish the world had joy.

Henry–Age 6

I wish to help children to don't do drugs.

Victor–Age 10

I wish I was very smart so I could solve everyones problems.

Christine–Age 9

I wish I could go back to the Tintanic and save it.

Nick–Age 8

I wish ereyone has to have freinds.

Shaila–Age 8

I wish I would have the bigest heart.

Andrew–Age 9

I wish that I somday make a diffrence.

Krystea–Age 9

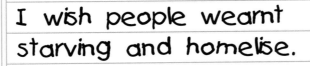

I wish people wearnt starving and homelise.

Hailie–Age 8

Book Endz

I wish I can be piced to be in the book.

Jaclyn–Age 7

I wish I will be faithful.

Jessica–Age 8

Atta girl Jaclyn! You were *picked!* I thank you and all the boys and girls who helped. I wish every one was in the book. As for your wish Jessica, I hope you're willing to share. I too wish to be faithful. I pray for children. I care about how they're treated and how many are not getting the love, support, joy and protection they need.

We are all student-teachers who are never too old to learn in the classroom of life. Children are great teachers. Being with them soothes my soul and allows me to right some wrongs from my own childhood. Sometimes, you're forced to take a risk yourself in order to be a protector for others. This book is such an example in my life. Having been there and done that, I've been asked to share some final thoughts and advice. Here is simply what works for me in connecting with children.

I view little ones as both young children and old souls. I admire their courage for coming back into the world at this time. I believe a child's soul remembers much more than their brain. This is why I talk to them (infants especially!) as if on some level, they totally understand what I'm saying. As I wrote at the opening of this book, I feel that *kids just know!* I feel I do, too.

I know kids crave healthy contact with grownups. They depend on it. So, I make sure I give them all the love, hugs, kisses, encouragement, compliments and reasons to laugh that I possibly can. I also listen to them and try to be present with them in whatever they're feeling in the moment. The more you give in life, the more you get. Never underestimate the power of a child! Please do appreciate the unique joy that can only be found in sharing your sacred human heart and soul in love with a child!

*Thanks for helping
to support children
and
children's charities!*

Kids Really Do Rule!

EASY ORDER FORM

Email Orders: orders@popdbooks.com.

Fax Orders: (866) 225-3742. Toll free. Send this form.

Telephone Orders: Call (866) 767-2665 (p-o-p-b-o-o-k). Toll free.
                         Be ready with your credit card information.

Mail Orders: Popular Demand Publishing, PO Box 16216,
                         Philadelphia, PA 19114-6216 USA

(*Use same information to book Thomas Baldrick for speaking
engagements, personal appearances and tailor-made seminars!)

Please Send Me: _____ copies of KIDS RULE! *The Hopes and
Dreams of 21st Century Children* at $14.95 each.

<small>I understand I may return books for a full refund within 30 days.</small>

Print Name: _____

Address: _____

City: _____

State: _____ Zip Code: _____

Telephone: _____

Email Address: _____

Payment: Credit Card   Check

(circle one)   Visa   MasterCard   Discover   Amex

Card Number: _____

Expiration Date: _____

Name On Card: _____

Sales Tax: Please add 7% for books shipped to Pennsylvania
                         address.

Shipping: $4 for 1st book (domestic).

Buy 3 . . . Get One Free!